World Black History

Independence *and* Equality

Elizabeth Cregan

Heinemann Library
Chicago, Illinois

www.heinemannraintree.com
Visit our website to find out more information about Heinemann-Raintree books.

To order:
☎ Phone 888-454-2279
💻 Visit www.heinemannraintree.com to browse our catalog and order online.

Edited by David Andrews, Louise Galpine, and Abby Colich
Designed by Ryan Frieson and Betsy Wernert
Illustrated by Mapping Specialists
Picture research by Mica Brancic
Originated by Heinemann Library
Printed in China by China Translation and Printing Services, Ltd.

13 12 11 10 09
10 9 8 7 6 5 4 3 2 1

Library of Congress Cataloging-in-Publication Data
Cregan, Elizabeth R.
  Independence and equality / Elizabeth Cregan. -- 1st ed.
    p. cm. -- (World black history)
  Includes bibliographical references and index.
  ISBN 978-1-4329-2387-7 (hc) -- ISBN 978-1-4329-2394-5 (pb) 1. Blacks--History--20th century--Juvenile literature. 2. African Americans--History--20th century--Juvenile literature. 3. Blacks--Civil rights--History--20th century--Juvenile literature. 4. African Americans--Civil rights--History--20th century--Juvenile literature. 5. African diaspora--History--20th century--Juvenile literature. 6. Race relations--History--20th century--Juvenile literature. 7. Racism--History--20th century--Juvenile literature. 8. Civil rights movements--History--20th century--Juvenile literature. 9. Independence movements--History--20th century--Juvenile literature. I. Title.
  DT16.5.C74 2009
  909'.0496082--dc22
                        2009003326

Acknowledgments

The author and publishers are grateful to the following for permission to reproduce copyrighted material: ©Corbis pp. **5** (Bettmann), **6** (Bettmann), **9**, **13** (Bettmann), **14** (Bettmann), **16** (Jack Moebes), **17** (Bettmann), **18** (Sygman/William Campbell), **24** (Hulton-Deutsch Collection), **32** (Sygma/Patrick Chauvel); ©Corbis Saba p. **37** (Louise Gubb); ©Getty Images pp. **4** (Keystone), **10** (New York Times Co.), **11** (MLB Photos), **12** (Time & Life Pictures/Carl Iwasaki), **15** (AFP/AFP), **19** (Time & Life Pictures/Robert W. Kelley), **20** (Keystone/Douglas Miller), **21** (Keystone), **22** (Knoote), **23** (Hulton Archive/Keystone), **25** (Express/Express), **26** (Hulton Archive), **27** (Time Life Pictures/Grey Villet), **29** (Popperfoto), **33** (Time Life Pictures/Terrence Spencer), **34** (Hulton Archive), **35** (Three Lions), **36** (Ejor), **39** (Hulton Archive), **40** (Terry Fincher), **41** (Michael Ochs Archives), **42** (Time Life Pictures/Alfred Eisenstaedt), **43** (Keystone/Reg Birkett); ©Imperial War Museum p. **30**; ©Naval Historical Foundation p. **7**; ©Rex Features p. **38** (Everett Collection).

Cover photograph of Martin Luther King, Jr., in March of 1965 leading a march from Selma, Alabama, to Montgomery, Alabama, to protest the lack of voting rights for African Americans. Beside King are John Lewis, Reverend Jesse Douglas, James Forman and Ralph Abernathy. Reproduced with permission of Corbis/© Steve Schapiro.

We would like to thank Marika Sherwood and Stephanie Davenport for their invaluable help in the preparation of this book.

Every effort has been made to contact copyright holders of any material reproduced in this book. Any omissions will be rectified in subsequent printings if notice is given to the publisher.

All the Internet addresses (URLs) given in this book were valid at the time of going to press. However, due to the dynamic nature of the Internet, some addresses may have changed, or sites may have changed or ceased to exist since publication. While the author and Publishers regret any inconvenience this may cause readers, no responsibility for any such changes can be accepted by either the author or the Publishers.

Contents

Some words are shown in bold, **like this**. You can find out what they mean by looking in the Glossary.

Seeking Freedom and Equality

The 1930s and 40s were a time of great change around the world. Nations such as the United States had gone from prosperity to **depression**. German leader Adolf Hitler attacked nations in Europe, sparking World War II (1939–1945).

However, for blacks around the world some things were still the same. Though in several countries they had made many advances since the days of slavery, blacks were still not truly free or equal.

For some the search for a better life meant moving to a new land. Many blacks left their homes in the Caribbean for Great Britain and the United States, but found that they were not always welcome.

A Racist Leader

Adolf Hitler led Germany by force and violence. This type of leader is called a **dictator**. Hitler was also a racist. He believed that whites were the superior race.

During this **protest** in London in 1959, racist slogans such as "Keep Britain White" let Black Britons know they were not welcome.

4

Discrimination Around the World

The world in 1940 was not an equal one. In the United States and elsewhere, signs of **racism** and **discrimination** were everywhere. A person's race impacted everything he or she did. African Americans went to separate schools and received lower paying jobs. Even simple activities, such as riding the bus or drinking from a water fountain, were **segregated**.

Many African Americans fought back by joining the **Civil Rights Movement**. They struggled to gain equal rights and put an end to racial discrimination and segregation.

Blacks around the world, from Brazil to India, worked for equality. In Africa, the land was divided into nations ruled by Europeans. Africans had to obey their European governors. They wanted to rule themselves. During the 1950s and 1960s, many African nations struggled to achieve independence.

By 1968 blacks in nations such as the United States and Great Britain had earned greater respect and more rights. Many African, and some Caribbean, nations had gained independence. But in many places, freedom and equality were still a dream.

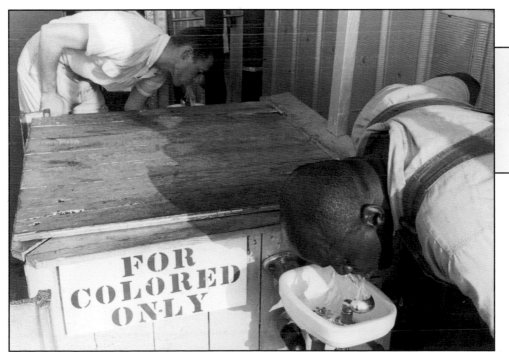

Even water fountains were segregated in the southern United States.

A World at War

In 1933 Adolf Hitler became the **dictator** of Germany. Germany was suffering a **depression** after losing World War I (1914–1918). Hitler promised to make things better. He managed to gain control of the government, and he put his **racist** views into action. He killed millions of **Jews** and others as he tried to create a world ruled by white Germans.

Hitler's army moved across Europe, conquering many countries. Italy and Japan joined forces with Hitler. By 1940 Great Britain was one of the only countries fighting the Nazis. Britain needed help to stop the German threat.

Following Japan's attack on the United States at Pearl Harbor, Hawaii, on December 7, 1941, the United States finally entered World War II. Among those fighting for the **Allies** were many African American soldiers. Many did not enjoy equal rights. For example, African Americans were not allowed to fight alongside white U.S. soldiers. Still, they were willing to risk their lives to preserve their nations' freedoms.

The Tuskegee Airmen, an African American unit, were decorated for their bravery in World War II.

Dorie Miller

Dorie Miller was a high school football player and a champion boxer in the U.S. Navy. But because he was black, the Navy would only let him help in the kitchen. He wasn't even trained to shoot a gun. During the Japanese attack on Pearl Harbor, Miller manned a large machine gun and shot down several Japanese planes. He was awarded the Navy Cross for bravery.

Black Soldiers, Sailors, and Airmen

When United States military leaders began recruiting people to serve in the war, African Americans were not a part of their plans. Of the 2.5 million African American men and women who signed up to join the military, less than half were invited to serve.

Thousands of blacks living in British colonies moved to Great Britain during World War II. Some worked in factories and in forestry. Others were accepted by the Royal Air Force, but the navy and army did not accept blacks. Thousands more fought for the British from their home countries in Africa and the Caribbean. France also recruited more than 100,000 black troops from its colonies.

Other Goals

Even in the military, blacks were not free from racial **discrimination**. They were given less important roles and treated differently than white soldiers.

Still, blacks hoped that helping win the war would earn them respect at home. Many African American soldiers hoped this new respect would change people's racist views. In the British colonies, many black fighters also hoped their service might lead to the independence of their homelands.

The Double V Campaign

African American writers wrote stories in newspapers arguing that the United States should fight two wars—against enemies at war and against racism at home. They believed that because blacks were fighting alongside whites, they should enjoy equal rights. They called this idea the Double V (for victory) Campaign.

Blood for Britain

The world's first **blood bank** drive, the World War II "Blood for Britain" drive, was conducted by African American doctor Charles Drew. Drew invented a new way of storing blood by separating it into parts. Using his new technique, blood could be stored much longer.

When World War II began, Drew worked to provide blood to the British Blood Bank. He became the first director of the American Red Cross Blood Bank. The British military also began using Drew's techniques to get blood to wounded soldiers at the front lines. With more blood available to the soldiers, many lives were saved in World War II.

Drew resigned when the government ordered the Red Cross to separate the blood taken from black and white people before sending it overseas. They wrongly believed blood from black people was different than blood from white people.

United We Win

The Double V Campaign helped people around the world see the discrimination many black people faced. Some even compared this unequal treatment to Hitler's racism. To fight this view, the United States government made movies and posters showing black and white soldiers working together. However, racial **segregation** in the military continued.

When the war ended in 1945, African American service men and women went home ready to fight for equal rights. Many had been awarded medals for their service, but segregation in the military continued until 1948.

Black British soldiers returning home from war were given little recognition or support. In Britain's colonies, those who had fought in the war saw no improvement in their lives. But the war experience taught them that Britain was not as powerful as it had been. They began to gain confidence that they could one day have independence.

Although the military was segregated, posters promoting the war effort often showed blacks and whites working together.

African Americans Stand Up

In 1945 southern African Americans faced some of the country's worst racial **discrimination**. In order to vote, they were required to pay **poll taxes** and take **literacy** tests.

Many African Americans had moved north and west to work in factories to support the war effort. There they could vote freely and improve their lives.

Southern African Americans had to enter movie theaters through a separate entrance.

But African Americans who stayed in the South suffered under **segregation**. Many schools, buses, restaurants, and drinking fountains were still marked "colored" or "white."

Many black veterans were angry. Even though they had shed blood fighting for America, they were still being treated like second-**class** citizens. Many southern whites believed these black veterans did not deserve equal rights. They tried to scare the veterans by beating and killing some of them.

John Johnson

John Johnson founded *Ebony* magazine in 1945. *Ebony* was filled with stories about African American life and culture. By showing the value of African American life, Johnson hoped his magazine would help fight **racism**.

The NAACP

By the end of World War II, black veterans in the United States and other African Americans began to focus on the fight for equal rights. One group leading the fight was the National Association for the Advancement of Colored People (NAACP).

The NAACP was formed in 1909 by black and white **civil rights** activists. They believed that all African Americans deserved equal rights. The NAACP did most of its fighting in the courts. NAACP lawyers argued cases of racial discrimination in housing and public places. They also fought to make it easier for African Americans to vote.

Jackie Robinson

One African American who defended his civil rights was Jackie Robinson. He left college to join the army to fight in World War II. Following the war, Robinson began his baseball career. At the time there were separate leagues for white and black players. Robinson was one of the top players in the all-black Negro League. In 1947 he joined the Brooklyn Dodgers and became the first black player on a Major League Baseball team. He became a great hitter, fielder, and base runner. After retiring from baseball, Robinson worked for the NAACP.

Brown v. Board of Education

During the 1940s and 1950s, thousands of people joined the NAACP to fight for equal rights. In 1951 some African Americans tried to enroll their children in all-white schools in Topeka, Kansas, but were stopped by city leaders. NAACP lawyers took their case, called *Brown v. Board of Education*, before the United States **Supreme Court** and won. The court said that every school must allow black and white children to go to school together.

Many white leaders in the southern states refused to obey this new law. Despite the court decisions, they kept their schools segregated.

Thurgood Marshall

Thurgood Marshall was an African American NAACP lawyer who won the *Brown v. Board of Education* case. Marshall also helped win rights for all Americans to live in any neighborhood they wished, to sit where they wanted on buses, and to vote freely. President Lyndon Johnson appointed Marshall the first African American to serve as a justice of the Supreme Court in 1967.

Black children in Topeka were segregated into separate schools, leading the NAACP to sue the school district.

Emmett Till's mother weeps as he is laid to rest in a Chicago cemetery.

"Look What They Did to My Boy"

Emmett Till was an African American teenager from Chicago, Illinois. Living in the northern United States, he was not used to the severe racial discrimination of the South. In 1955 on a visit to see his Uncle Moses in Mississippi, Emmett was accused of whistling at a white woman. Three days later, two white men dragged Emmett out of bed. They beat him, wrapped his body in barbed wire, and tossed him in a river.

Newspapers and magazines around the world covered Emmett's funeral. His mother decided to have an open casket funeral so the world could see what they did to her boy. The men accused of killing Emmett were set free. Later they confessed their guilt to a magazine reporter. The men never went to jail for their crime.

Following the murder of Emmett Till, the **Civil Rights Movement** spread quickly across America.

13

The Fight for Civil Rights

If two white people could murder a black teenage boy and not face punishment, how could African Americans ever win the fight for equal rights? The NAACP was determined to find a way. They found their opportunity to fight **segregation** in Montgomery, Alabama, with the help of Rosa Parks, a seamstress and NAACP member.

The Montgomery Bus Boycott

In Montgomery, African Americans had to sit in the back of city buses. After work on December 1, 1955, Parks got on a bus and took a seat in the front. As the bus filled up, the driver ordered Parks to get up and make way for a white man.

Parks refused to move. She was arrested, and her actions started the Montgomery Bus **Boycott**. The Reverend Martin Luther King, Jr., led this **protest**. Rather than ride city buses, African Americans used carpools to get around. They went to mass meetings for support. Finally, in 1956, the **Supreme Court** outlawed segregation on buses.

Following a 1956 Supreme Court decision outlawing segregation in buses, Rosa Parks takes a seat at the front of a bus.

The Little Rock Nine

Leaders in many southern states ignored the Supreme Court's decisions. African Americans still had to sit in the back of city buses and attend all-black schools. There were only three school districts with racially mixed classrooms. One was in Texas and two were in Arkansas.

Many Americans wanted things to change much faster. Once again, the NAACP stepped in. In Little Rock, Arkansas, they helped nine teenagers enroll in the all-white Central High School.

A Tense Confrontation

When the students tried to go to school, groups that favored segregation blocked the entrance. The governor of Arkansas, Orval Faubus, sent the National Guard to stop the students. Eventually, local police brought the students in, which led to rioting. The students still went to school, even though other students spat on them and called them names.

Federal troops were brought in by President Eisenhower to protect African American students as they enter Central High School in Little Rock, Arkansas, in 1957.

The next year, the governor closed all the schools rather than allow racial **integration**. A year later, after more court rulings, the schools were forced to reopen as integrated schools.

Peaceful Protests

By the late 1950s, Dr. Martin Luther King was a leader of the **Civil Rights Movement**. Dr. King believed in peaceful protests. This attracted many college students. They traveled all over the South helping blacks register to vote. They also invented a new kind of protest: the **sit-in**.

King and Gandhi

Dr. King got many of his ideas from Mahatma Gandhi (1869–1948). Gandhi was an Indian leader who helped his country peacefully win independence from Britain. He also led peaceful protests to help Indians in South Africa win equal rights.

The students thought it was unfair that blacks were not allowed to eat with whites. On February 1, 1960, four young black men sat at a "white" lunch counter in Greensboro, North Carolina. Nobody served them, but the young men sat in their seats all day.

Both black and white students joined the sit-in. An angry crowd of local whites also gathered. They yelled at the students and threw drinks on them. Soon sit-ins were happening all over the South.

Black students stage a sit-in at a "white" lunch counter in Greensboro, North Carolina.

Freedom Riders

Segregation on buses was illegal, but some states did not enforce the law. A **civil rights** group called Congress for Racial Equality (CORE) decided to test the law. In May of 1961, they sent a group of blacks and whites on a bus trips through the South, from Washington, D.C., to New Orleans, Louisiana. This journey was called the "Freedom Ride."

The first part of their trip was peaceful. But when they got to Alabama, one bus was bombed. As the riders got off the bus, a mob of angry white people attacked them. Many Freedom Riders were hurt.

The United States government ordered the Alabama governor to protect the freedom riders. State police protected them at first, but then disappeared, and more riders were attacked. Finally state and federal troops were sent in to protect the riders.

In Mississippi many riders were sent to jail for trespassing. But CORE just kept sending more riders to board the buses.

Voting Rights

The law said that African Americans had the right to vote. Black children had the right to go to school with white children. African Americans also had the right to sit anywhere on a city bus. But in the South, white leaders ignored these laws.

Many southern states charged a **poll tax**, a special tax all voters had to pay. Voters also had to pass a **literacy** test in order to vote. But since most African Americans were very poor and lacked education, they were not able to vote. These rules also stopped many poor whites from voting.

If black voters managed to pay the poll tax and pass the test, some Southern whites threatened to beat or kill them if they voted.

The Ku Klux Klan

Members of the society of the Ku Klux Klan wanted to stop African Americans from voting. They would cover their faces with white hoods and robes, and burn crosses in the front yard of anyone who supported African American rights.

Hooded members of the Ku Klux Klan often burned crosses to scare anyone who supported equal rights for African Americans.

"I Have a Dream"

During the 1960s, it was still hard for most African Americans to find good jobs. Black families made a little more than half as much money as white families. Black leaders wanted to show the country that African Americans were tired of waiting for fair treatment. So they organized a march in Washington, D.C.

On August 28, 1963, over 190,000 black and 60,000 white Americans marched for racial equality. In a famous speech, Dr. Martin Luther King said:

> I have a dream that my four little children will one day live in a nation where they will not be judged by the color of their skin, but by the content of their character.

New Laws for Equality

The Civil Rights Act became law in 1964, and the Voting Rights Law was passed in 1965. These laws made all racial **discrimination** illegal. They stopped the poll taxes and literacy tests that kept blacks from voting. But the fight for equality was far from over.

Britain's Windrush Generation

After World War II, the British government invited people from all over the empire to help rebuild the country. They needed workers for the low paying, unskilled jobs no one else would do. Since many blacks living in British colonies were very poor and needed jobs, they accepted this invitation. In 1948, 492 black men from Jamaica arrived in Great Britain aboard the ship *Empire Windrush*.

Many of these men had fought for Great Britain during the war. Even so, they were not welcomed. Because of **discrimination** and a lack of housing, the white British sent many of the Windrush men away when they tried to find places to stay. The **racism** they encountered made the Windrush men angry. They began to speak out and fight to gain equal rights to housing and better jobs.

Many blacks from Caribbean colonies, including those who had fought for Great Britain in the war, remained in Britain. There was little work for them back home.

The *Empire Windrush* arrives in England with 498 Jamaicans on board.

One sign of racism in Britain was the "colour bar," an unofficial rule that prevented Black Britons from gaining the same jobs as whites.

Strangers in Their Own Country

The arrival of the *Empire Windrush* started a wave of British immigration. Many immigrants seeking work arrived from British colonies in Africa and the Caribbean, as well as from India. They hoped to earn money to send home to their families.

In 1948 the British government passed a law offering citizenship to people from the colonies. But the British people did not welcome them as equals.

They were afraid that these black immigrants would take their jobs and homes. They tried to keep blacks out of their lives. Many were denied housing and good jobs, and children were treated badly at school. They felt like strangers in what they had been taught was their "Mother Country."

Learie Constantine

Blacks were not allowed to stay at many hotels in Great Britain. This practice was one effect of "the colour bar." Learic Constantine was a former cricket player from Trinidad who worked for the government. In 1943, while in London for a meeting, he tried to stay in a hotel but was sent away. Learie took the hotel to court and won his case. Later he became the first Black British citizen appointed to the **House of Lords**.

The Notting Hill Riots

By the end of the 1950s, Great Britain was home to 192,000 blacks. Most of the newcomers settled in cities. London's Notting Hill neighborhood was one area where black immigrants could find places to live.

In 1958 the British economy weakened. Jobs became hard to find and tensions grew between the black and white communities. Whites attacked blacks in London and in other major cities.

In August of that year, riots broke out in Notting Hill and in the city of Nottingham, north of London. Groups of white teenagers attacked West Indian immigrants and destroyed their property. White adults joined in the attacks. Many accused the immigrants of taking the scarce jobs and housing available after the war.

Conflicts Over Immigration

The riots led the British government to restrict immigration. Some hoped to limit **racial diversity**, though they claimed to be only concerned about preserving jobs. The new laws angered many black immigrants.

In the spring of 1959, a black carpenter named Kelso Cochrane, from the Caribbean island of Antigua, was stabbed to death while walking home in Notting Hill. The police were told that white youths murdered Cochrane. Perhaps hoping to prevent more rioting, the police concluded that the murders were not motivated by racism.

Racial discrimination continued. Some whites even claimed that black school children were less intelligent than whites. Many Black Britons began to work against racial inequality by forming both self-help and campaigning organizations.

The murder of Kelso Cochrane has never been solved.

Claudia Jones

Claudia Jones was a civil rights activist born in Trinidad. She traveled throughout the United States giving speeches on women's rights and racial issues. After spending time in prison for her **communist** views, she was sent to Britain in 1955. Jones founded several organizations and continued to speak out against discrimination. In 1958 she started the *West Indian Gazette*, a newspaper dedicated to ending discrimination and **imperialism**.

Gaining Full Citizenship

During the 1960s, many Black Britons began to leave the poor neighborhoods of large cities like London for smaller cities and suburbs. They found better jobs and homes. At the same time, more new immigrants arrived from around the world. By 1962 there were more than 362,000 Black Britons.

Then new immigration laws were passed. Only immigrants who had been promised jobs, or who had served in World War II, could enter. The wives and children of those already settled were also allowed to enter. In 1968 these restrictions expanded. People from former British colonies who had British passports, who had been previously been allowed to immigrate, now were banned unless they had a grandparent born in Britain.

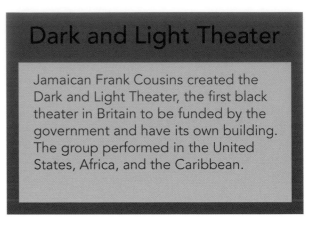

Dark and Light Theater

Jamaican Frank Cousins created the Dark and Light Theater, the first black theater in Britain to be funded by the government and have its own building. The group performed in the United States, Africa, and the Caribbean.

Some Black Britons joined new organizations such as the Campaign Against Racial Discrimination to fight for the end of discrimination.

Immigrants arrive in Southampton, England, from the West Indies in 1961.

Race Relations Acts

As racial discrimination continued, so did **protests** by blacks. Some whites also continued to protest. Small-scale riots were spreading throughout the country. The government was forced to act.

Beginning in 1965, the government passed a series of laws aimed at ending discrimination and improving race relations. In 1965 a Race Relations Board was formed. This board enforced rules against discrimination. However, the board had few powers to act. The Community Relations Council, set up in 1968, was also weak and ineffective.

In 1976 these groups were replaced with the Commission for Racial Equality. This commission outlawed discrimination in the workplace, schools, housing, and other areas. Citizens were allowed to take their cases to court if discrimination occurred. Even with these new laws in place, racial discrimination continued.

Enoch Powell

One member of **Parliament** who opposed the Race Relations Acts was Enoch Powell. Powell delivered an angry speech warning that allowing immigration would result in rivers "foaming with much blood." He claimed that his **constituents** were worried that "in fifteen or twenty years' time the black man will have the whip hand over the white man."

Powell was disciplined for his speech, but many people shared his views. They held rallies to support Powell and to protest continued immigration.

Freedom in the Caribbean and South America

Life in the Caribbean colonies was often harsh. Many blacks were poor and few were able to find jobs. Thousands had moved to the United States or Great Britain in search of opportunity. Others moved to Panama to help build the Panama Canal.

For the millions who stayed behind, life was poor and jobs were hard to find. The struggle for independence seemed like an uphill battle. But Barbados is one nation that succeeded.

Opportunities in Barbados

Like many Caribbean colonies, Barbados was developed by African slaves. In 1833 the British **Parliament** declared that slaves would be freed, but only after serving as apprentices for several years. The slaves revolted and were granted full freedom in 1838. However, whites owned all the land. The free blacks had no choice but to work on farms for whites or to leave the country.

When they won their freedom in 1833, former slaves marched through the streets of Barbados in celebration.

Finally, in the early 1900s, Caribbean blacks began forming "Friendly Societies" to improve the lives of blacks. These organizations would help the families of black workers who fell ill or died. The societies bought land to help the workers gain better incomes. Blacks finally gained some power.

Gaining Independence

While blacks in Barbados were making progress, white landowners still controlled most of the country. In 1934 they formed the Barbados Produce Exporters Association. This group secretly agreed to pay black workers lower wages. Some black workers went on strike in **protest**. One demonstration in 1937 ended in 14 deaths.

Black activist Grantley Adams and others worked to support the black workers. Adams was a lawyer and member of the **Barbados House of Assembly**. The government sent him to England to discuss the racial problems. He told English leaders they could avoid riots if they helped improve conditions for black workers.

In 1938 workers formed the Barbados Labour Party. They elected Adams as their leader. Adams fought for new laws that led to many improvements for Black Barbadians. These laws gave black workers the right to vote, better health care, improved schools, and a minimum wage.

Activist Grantley Adams, head of the Barbados Labour Party, helped Barbadians achieve their independence from Great Britain.

In 1961 Great Britain granted Barbados the right to rule itself. Barbados became an independent state on November 30, 1966.

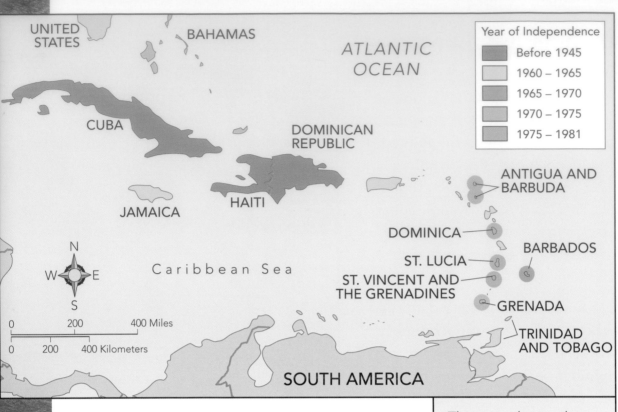

This map shows when each Caribbean nation won its independence.

Year of Independence
- Before 1945
- 1960 – 1965
- 1965 – 1970
- 1970 – 1975
- 1975 – 1981

Caribbean Independence

During the 1950s and 1960s, many other British colonies in the Caribbean struggled to achieve independence. In 1958 a group of island colonies joined together to form the West Indies Federation. The colonies hoped that forming this single body would help them achieve their independence from Great Britain.

The Federation hoped to achieve independence by 1962. But the colonies disagreed on many things. Jamaica, the largest and richest member, feared it would have to support the others and left the group in 1961. Then Trinidad and Tobago left the Federation. The Federation was dissolved in 1962. Jamaica and Trinidad and Tobago were granted independence in 1962. Other colonies would have to wait several years to be free of British rule.

CARIFTA Forms

The Caribbean Free Trade Association (CARIFTA) was formed in 1968. It replaced the West Indies Federation. It helped Caribbean nations work together to sell goods and create jobs. Members of CARIFTA hoped their work would improve the lives of people in the Caribbean.

Inequality in Brazil

Brazil is home to the largest black population outside of Africa. A majority of its 170 million citizens can trace their roots to Africa. The Portuguese brought millions of black slaves to Brazil to develop the land.

Even though slavery was abolished in 1888, there are still few Black Brazilian leaders. Most never go to school beyond the sixth grade and work as unskilled, poorly paid laborers.

In 1931 black leaders formed the Black Brazilian Front. They worked for equal rights, but were shut down when **fascist** leaders came to power. The fascists encouraged immigration of whites to Brazil to "whiten" the population.

Today, **discrimination** is illegal in Brazil, but it still exists in many forms. Little progress has been made in the struggle for equality.

Pelé

Perhaps the greatest soccer player of all time was Black Brazilian player Edson Arantes do Nascimento, known as Pelé. He grew up in poverty and earned extra money by shining shoes. Pelé's father taught him to play soccer, and he practiced using a stuffed sock. By the age of 15, he had joined a professional team, and soon he was the league's top scorer.

Pelé joined Brazil's national team in 1957, when he was 16. He became the youngest person to play in the World Cup, and scored six goals in leading Brazil to win the cup. He played in three more World Cups, with Brazil winning the championship twice. During his career he scored 1,281 goals, the highest total ever.

Pelé also dedicated himself to other causes. With the United Nations, he worked to preserve the environment. He also spoke out against **racism** and poverty in Brazil. When he scored his 1,000th goal, he dedicated it to the poor children of Brazil.

African Independence

During World War II, all African nations except Liberia were ruled by European countries. Africa was rich in manpower and natural resources, such as rubber and minerals. Great Britain and its **allies** needed these resources to fight the war. So did their enemies, Germany and Italy.

Fighting for Resources

In 1935 Italian **dictator** Benito Mussolini invaded Ethiopia. This news angered many Africans, so when World War II began, many were willing to fight against Germany and Italy. Others were forced by local chiefs to work in the mines and on farms to help with the war effort.

Britain needed metals such as tin to build weapons. They turned to their African colonies, forcing Nigerian miners to work under terrible conditions. In the Belgian Congo, forced labor and the high cost of living led to mining strikes in 1941. The miners were forced back to work, and 70 were killed.

Movement to End Imperial Rule

When Africans returned home after the war, they had a hard time finding jobs. After fighting in the war, they felt they had earned better lives and more rights. Soon, Africans were fighting to end imperial rule across Africa.

African soldiers remove stones that once marked the border between Kenya and the Italian colony of Somaliland in 1941.

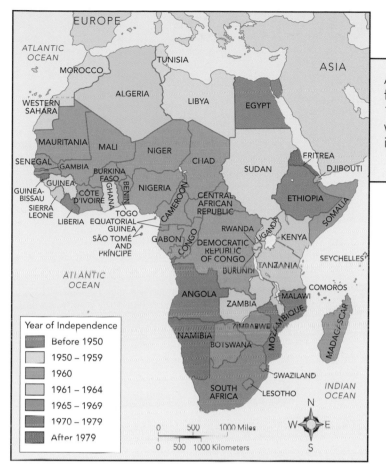

EUROPE
ATLANTIC OCEAN
MOROCCO
TUNISIA
ASIA
ALGERIA
LIBYA
EGYPT
WESTERN SAHARA
MAURITANIA
MALI
NIGER
CHAD
SUDAN
ERITREA
SENEGAL
GAMBIA
BURKINA FASO
DJIBOUTI
GUINEA-BISSAU
GUINEA
GHANA
BENIN
NIGERIA
CAMEROON
CENTRAL AFRICAN REPUBLIC
ETHIOPIA
SIERRA LEONE
CÔTE D'IVOIRE
TOGO
SOMALIA
LIBERIA
EQUATORIAL GUINEA
RWANDA
UGANDA
KENYA
SÃO TOMÉ AND PRÍNCIPE
GABON
CONGO
DEMOCRATIC REPUBLIC OF CONGO
BURUNDI
TANZANIA
SEYCHELLES
ATLANTIC OCEAN
ANGOLA
ZAMBIA
MALAWI
COMOROS
MOZAMBIQUE
MADAGASCAR
NAMIBIA
ZIMBABWE
BOTSWANA
SWAZILAND
INDIAN OCEAN
SOUTH AFRICA
LESOTHO

Year of Independence
- Before 1950
- 1950 – 1959
- 1960
- 1961 – 1964
- 1965 – 1969
- 1970 – 1979
- After 1979

0   500   1000 Miles
0   500   1000 Kilometers

N W E S

All African nations were free of colonial rule by 1993. This map shows when each nation won its independence.

The Pan-African Movement

Black activists in the United States and the Caribbean started a movement in the 1900s to bring Africans together. This came to be called the Pan-African Movement. In 1945 the Fifth Pan-African Congress was held in Manchester, England. It called for the end of colonial rule in African nations.

Weakened by Colonial Rule

Africa had been weakened by the slave trade, colonial rule, and a long world war. Colonial rulers controlled all of Africa's banks and most other businesses. Their main goal was to export goods, not help the country. Some Africans were educated in Europe and America. But when they returned home, they were only offered low-level government jobs. They had few chances to become leaders or administrators.

All African nations were made up of hundreds of different **ethnic** groups. Each group of people had its own way of life. Most spoke different languages and had different legal, religious, and government traditions. This made it very hard to work together for independence.

Violent Independence Movements

Despite the challenges, African nations won their independence. Some of their struggles for independence were bloody. Others were not. Some of the most violent independence movements were in the former Portuguese colonies of Angola, Mozambique, Guinea Bissau, and São Tomé.

These colonies sought to win independence peacefully. But the Portuguese refused to give up control. There were many armed conflicts. When Portuguese forces finally left in 1974 and 1975, they abandoned the continent quickly, without preparing an orderly transition. In Angola rival forces fought for control for more than 25 years, leaving hundreds of thousands dead.

African Nations Unite

In 1963 all African nations, both free and colonized, joined together to form the Organization of African Unity (OAU). The OAU helped eliminate colonial rule. It worked to help Africans achieve basic human rights and a better standard of living. The OAU also helped settle conflicts between African nations. It was renamed the African Union in 2002.

Soldiers in Angola fought for independence in a bloody civil war.

Revolt in Kenya

In 1952 a group in Kenya known as the Land of Freedom Army fought the British to take back their land and farms. This uprising was known around the world as the Mau Mau Revolt.

The British arrested several Kenyan leaders, accusing them of helping the uprising. One was Jomo Kenyatta, the head of the Kenya African Union, an organization formed in 1944 to push for independence. He denied working with the rebels, but was sent to prison for nine years. However, the revolt spread. The rebels attacked many white settlers and some of their own chiefs, who were helping the British.

Jomo Kenyatta was elected Kenya's first president in 1963.

Ending the Uprising

The British brought in thousands of troops to stop the uprising. Nearly 12,000 Kenyans were killed. The British defeated the rebels in 1956.

The British tried to improve conditions for the Kenyans. They raised wages and held free elections of local government leaders. But it took many soldiers to keep the peace. Britain finally granted Kenya its independence in 1963. Jomo Kenyatta was its first president.

The Belgian Congo

The Belgian Congo's path to independence was also violent. This colony was rich in mineral resources. The United States and European nations had set up copper, gold, tin, and diamond mines.

The Belgian rulers made little effort to develop the country. The country had few educated leaders. There were only 19 college graduates in the entire country.

The Belgians refused to discuss independence with Congolese leaders. In 1959 rioting broke out. The following year Belgium announced it would allow the election of a local leader to rule the country.

This sudden decision caused much confusion. Many political parties were formed across the Congo to take part in the election. But only one wanted a central government. This group was led by a man named Patrice Lumumba. In 1960 Lumumba was elected to lead the independent Congo nation.

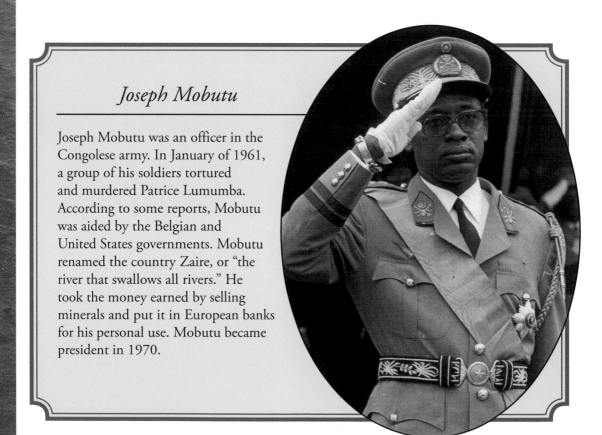

Joseph Mobutu

Joseph Mobutu was an officer in the Congolese army. In January of 1961, a group of his soldiers tortured and murdered Patrice Lumumba. According to some reports, Mobutu was aided by the Belgian and United States governments. Mobutu renamed the country Zaire, or "the river that swallows all rivers." He took the money earned by selling minerals and put it in European banks for his personal use. Mobutu became president in 1970.

More Peaceful Paths to Independence

By 1956 all French colonies in West Africa governed themselves in some ways. But France still controlled the military and made all the decisions for the nations' economies.

In 1958 France's President Charles de Gaulle offered these colonies a choice. They could continue under French rule or they could break away. He warned that if a colony wanted to break away, all support would end.

Guinea Breaks Away

The only West African colony to break away from France was Guinea. The leader of Guinea, Sékou Touré, told France that Guinea wanted complete independence.

France sent all government workers home. They emptied out office files and ripped out the telephones. Touré continued to lead his people, and Guinea earned independence in 1959.

Though at first a **socialist**, Touré ended up ruling Guinea as a **dictator**. He did not allow his citizens to speak freely and arrested many opponents. After he died in 1984, dictators continued to rule Guinea.

Sékou Touré ruled the nation of Guinea as a dictator.

Separation in South Africa

In South Africa, the policy of **apartheid** separated citizens by race. Beginning in 1948, nonwhites—black South Africans, Asians, and others— were officially considered a lower **class** than whites. Blacks were deemed the lowest of all the races.

Under apartheid, black South Africans were moved to separate areas apart from whites. These areas were poorer and less developed, with poorer land, schools, and job opportunities. Blacks could not vote or run for office. They could only go into the white areas if they were working there, or if they had a special paper called a passbook.

Many black South Africans fought to end apartheid. One was a young lawyer named Nelson Mandela. He led the African National Congress (ANC) in the fight to end apartheid. The ANC wanted to reach all South Africans. They organized strikes and **protests**. Mandela and hundreds of other black South Africans burned their passbooks in protest.

This sign warns white South Africans to beware of black Africans in the area.

Ending Apartheid

Mandela called for equal rights and full citizenship for black South Africans. Under his leadership, the African National Congress protested. They refused to carry their passbooks. They went into the restricted "whites only" areas and kept their children home from "black only" schools. In 1964 Mandela and many of his fellow activists were arrested and sent to Robben Island Prison.

In prison the men spent their days breaking rocks into small pieces. The white guards tossed the rocks into the ocean at the end of the day. But Mandela and the other prisoners did not give up. The prisoners demanded better food and clothes.

Around the world, people heard what was happening. Many people protested the apartheid system. Mandela was finally freed in 1990. In 1994 he was elected South Africa's first black president. This free election marked the end of apartheid.

African Americans Struggle On

Dr. Martin Luther King, Jr., believed that peaceful **protests** were the best way to achieve equality. But not everyone agreed. Many African Americans were frustrated by continuing **racism**. Leaders in the South ignored laws granting equal rights. Most African Americans still made less money than whites and were treated poorly.

A group of black and white students formed the Student Nonviolent Coordinating Committee (SNCC). In the early 1960s, SNCC and other **civil rights** groups began registering black voters across Mississippi. Whites tried to stop their efforts through intimidation and violence. In June of 1964, three SNCC students were murdered—two white and one black. But only a few students quit. The rest kept on registering voters.

Stokely Carmichael

Born in Trinidad, Stokely Carmichael was a leader of SNCC and a Freedom Rider (see page 17). He believed that African Americans should create a distinct identity from other Americans—from separate communities to distinct hairstyles. His slogan was "Black is beautiful." He also spoke in favor of "Black Power"—the idea that African Americans should have racial pride and be independent of whites. Unlike Martin Luther King, he believed blacks should seek equality by any means, including violence if necessary.

Malcolm X

As a child, Malcolm Little didn't seem to be destined for great things. After his father, a civil rights activist, was killed, he lived in foster homes. He was a good student, but eventually he turned to crime. He was convicted of burglary and sent to prison in 1947. In prison he began to educate himself. Malcolm would read through the night.

Malcolm's brother convinced him to join the Nation of Islam (NOI), a black religious group. He changed his last name from "Little" to "X." The X was a symbol of his lost name from Africa. When Malcolm was released from prison in 1952, he became a minister for the NOI.

Malcolm was a powerful speaker. He convinced many African Americans that peaceful protests would not help. He believed that blacks and whites should be separate. He said, "I believe in the brotherhood of man, all men, but I don't believe in brotherhood with someone who doesn't want brotherhood with me." He believed that when faced with violence, blacks should not be afraid to fight back with violence.

Malcolm's speeches helped the Nation of Islam grow. After a disagreement with NOI leaders, Malcolm formed his own group. In 1965, after receiving death threats from the NOI, Malcolm X was murdered.

Thousands of African Americans served in the Vietnam War.

The Vietnam War

In the 1960s, the United States became deeply involved in a war in Vietnam. The goal of the war was to prevent **communist** forces from taking over South Vietnam. A higher percentage of African Americans served in Vietnam than in any previous American war. At the height of the Vietnam War in 1969, about 12 percent of the soldiers in Vietnam were black. Between 1961 and 1966, African Americans made up more than 20 percent of the combat-related deaths in the army.

The United States' participation in the Vietnam War grew at the same time the **Civil Rights Movement** swept the country. Civil rights leaders were outraged by the military's **draft** policies, which resulted in many African Americans fighting and dying in combat. Few African Americans served on draft boards, the groups that helped decide who would be drafted.

Dr. Martin Luther King, Jr., led many **protests** against the Vietnam War. He believed that the United States was trying to unjustly occupy Vietnam. He also described the war as **racist**—"a white man's war, a black man's fight."

The Death of Martin Luther King

In March of 1968, Dr. King went to Memphis, Tennessee, to support a protest of black workers demanding equal pay and better working conditions. As he stood on the balcony outside his motel room, a single bullet fired by a white man named James Earl Ray struck King. He was rushed to the hospital, where he died.

News of King's death spread around the world. A wave of rioting erupted in over 100 cities in the United States. President Johnson declared a national day of mourning. A crowd of 300,000 attended his funeral.

After Dr. King

The **assassination** of Martin Luther King changed the Civil Rights Movement. There were fewer mass protests, but progress was being made. In April of that year, President Johnson signed a law making it illegal to practice racial **discrimination** in the sale or rental of housing. New leaders like Jesse Jackson and Shirley Chisolm ran for President and worked to help African Americans help themselves.

Thousands attended the funeral of Dr. Martin Luther King.

41

Free at Last?

Many new laws were passed to protect African Americans from **discrimination**. They finally had all the same rights as whites. They could vote freely, so more black leaders were voted into office. Many African Americans moved from the South to the North and West. They held better jobs and could afford to live in better homes and neighborhoods.

But life did not improve for all African Americans. Many still held low-paying jobs and lived in **ghettos** such as Harlem in New York, the south and west sides of Chicago, and Watts in Los Angeles.

In his "I Have a Dream" speech, Martin Luther King, Jr., imagined a time when blacks and whites could join hands and say they were all "free at last." But in 1970 racial discrimination remained.

African American Studies

In 1969 black students protested because no classes focused on their culture and history. Soon San Francisco State University began offering Black Studies classes. African American studies and Black studies spread to schools across the country.

Howard University was one of many universities to offer classes in African American studies.

Closer to Equality

Great Britain's Race Relations Act made discrimination illegal. Black Britons could live in the same places, work at the same jobs, and attend the same schools as whites. As opportunities grew, their lives began to improve.

But most Black Britons continued to face racial discrimination. Many lived in poor, inner city areas. Many whites still did not welcome them in their neighborhoods.

Rocky Paths to a Better Life

Most African nations were independent by 1968. For many nations, the challenges of developing a new country, with diverse peoples and limited resources, would prove very difficult.

Several independent African and Caribbean nations, such as Uganda and Haiti, fell into the hands of **dictators**. Many others were troubled by corruption. Most blacks in the Caribbean were very poor, surviving by growing food on their own land.

By 1968 blacks around the world had made great progress toward a life of equality and prosperity. But much work remained.

Gold Coast Cadets celebrate Ghana's new independence at the embassy in Belgrave Square in 1957.

Timeline

1939   Germany attacks Poland. World War II begins.

1940   Dr. Charles Drew discovers a way to store blood and create blood banks.

1941   The United States joins World War II. African Americans begin to move from the South to the North and West to work in factories supporting the war effort.

1942   The Congress of Racial Equality (CORE) is founded in Chicago, Illinois.

1943   The Detroit Race Riot claims the lives of 25 African Americans.

1943   Caribbean cricket player Learie Constantine and his family are turned away from London hotel because they are black.

1944   Great Britain signs an agreement granting independence to the African nation of Ethiopia.

1945   World War II ends. Millions of blacks soldiers, sailors, and pilots return home.

1947   Jackie Robinson becomes the first African American athlete to play Major League Baseball.

1948   The *Empire Windrush* arrives in Great Britain with 492 black workers from the West Indies aboard.

1948   Great Britain passes a law offering citizenship to its colonial subjects.

1951   The African nation of Libya wins its independence from Italy.

1954   The U.S. Supreme Court rules in *Brown v. Board of Education* that black and white children must be able to go to school together.

1955   Fourteen-year-old Emmett Till is lynched in Money, Mississippi.

1955   Rosa Parks refuses to give up her bus seat to a white man, beginning the Montgomery Bus **Boycott**.

1956   The African nation of Tunisia wins its independence from France. Sudan wins its independence from Great Britain.

1957   United States President Eisenhower sends troops to Little Rock, Arkansas, to protect the Little Rock Nine.

1957   The African nation of Morocco wins its independence from France, and Ghana wins its independence from Great Britain.

1958   The Notting Hill Riots break out in London, England.

1958   The African nation of Guinea wins its independence from France.

1958   The West Indies Federation is formed.

1959   A Black West Indian carpenter named Kelso Cochrane is stabbed to death while walking home in Notting Hill, London.

1960	Four students begin a **sit-in** at a lunch counter in North Carolina to protest the ban against serving blacks.
1960	African nations Congo, Gabon, Ivory Coast, French-ruled Cameroon, and Mauritania win their independence from France; Zaire from Belgium; Somalia from Italy and Great Britain; and Nigeria from Great Britain.
1961	The Congress of Racial Equality organizes Freedom Rides in the southern United States.
1961	Great Britain grants the island nation Barbados the right to rule itself.
1961	The African nations Chad, Central African Republic, Sierra Leone, British-ruled Cameroon, and Tanganyika (which joined with Zanzibar to become Tanzania in 1964) all win their independence from Great Britain.
1962	More African nations win their independence: Togo, Senegal, Mali, Madagascar, Benin, Niger, Burkina Faso, Burundi, and Rwanda from Belgium; Algeria from France; and Uganda from Great Britain.
1963	Over 200,000 people gather in Washington, D.C., to demand equal rights for African Americans. Dr. Martin Luther King, Jr., delivers his "I Have a Dream" speech.
1963	The African nations of Tanzania and Kenya win their independence from Great Britain.
1964	Three **civil rights** workers are murdered in Mississippi.
1964	Nelson Mandela is sent to prison for fighting to end **apartheid** in South Africa.
1964	The African nations Zambia and Swaziland win their independence from Great Britain.
1965	The African nation Gambia wins its independence from Great Britain.
1965	Malcolm X is shot to death while giving a speech in New York City.
1966	Stokely Carmichael becomes the leader of the Student Non-violent Coordinating Committee (SNCC).
1966	Barbados becomes an independent state.
1966	The African nations Botswana and Lesotho win their independence from Great Britain.
1967	Thurgood Marshall takes his seat as the first African American judge on the United States **Supreme Court**.
1968	Dr. Martin Luther King is killed in Memphis, Tennessee.
1968	The African nation of Mauritius wins its independence from Great Britain. Equatorial Guinea becomes independent of Spain.

Glossary

Allies countries who joined together to fight in World War II, included the United States, Great Britain, and France. The allies fought against the Axis powers.

apartheid former South African laws that segregated whites and blacks

assassination murder of a leader

Barbados House of Assembly the lower-ranking body of the Barbados government

blood bank storage space for donated blood to give to injured people

boycott to refuse to deal with a person or group because you do not agree with them

civil rights rights of citizens to be treated fairly and equally in all aspects of civic life

Civil Rights Movement a series of movements from 1955 to 1968 in the United States aimed at ending racial discrimination

class a group sharing the same status in a community. A community can have several different levels of classes.

communist a political belief in which property and goods are held in common

constituent resident of an area who is served by a government representative

depression long period of economic hardship

dictator a person who rules by force and violence

discrimination treating people differently due to race, gender, or other factors

draft system of randomly selecting citizens to serve in the military during war

ethnic relating to a group of people, such as its culture, customs, and traditions

fascist a form of dictatorship which believes that some races are better than others

ghetto a part of a city that is usually poor and is made up mainly of people of one race or ethnic group

House of Lords the second chamber of the British Parliament

imperialism the act of one nation controlling smaller or weaker nations

integration mixing people of different races or ethnic groups

Jew a person whose religion is Judaism

literacy the ability to read and write

parliament British governing body that is made up of two houses, the House of Commons and the House of Lords

poll tax a tax every citizen paid in order to vote. Poll taxes were outlawed in the United States in 1965.

protest to complain and tell someone that you do not agree with them

racial diversity people of different races being represented in one place

racism the belief that certain races of people are better than others

segregation to keep a group or race of people separate or apart

sit-in a type of peaceful protest in which people occupy a space and refuse to move

socialist economic system in which wealth is shared

Supreme Court the highest court of law in the United States

Find Out More

Books

Buckley, James. *Pelé.* New York: DK, 2007.

DeGezelle, Terri. *Rosa Parks and the Civil Rights Movement.* Chicago: Heinemann Library, 2008.

Martin, Jennifer, *Apartheid in South Africa.* Farmington Hills, Mich.: Lucent, 2006.

Price, Sean. *When Will I Get In? Segregation and Civil Rights.* Chicago: Raintree, 2007.

Websites

From Slavery to Freedom: Africans in the Americas
http://hhsu.learning.hhs.gov/slaverytofreedom/

International Civil Rights Center and Museum
http://www.sitinmovement.org/history.html

PBS American Experience: Eyes on the Prize: America's Civil Rights Movement 1954–1985
http://www.pbs.org/wgbh/amex/eyesontheprize/

Index